W9-ASJ-859

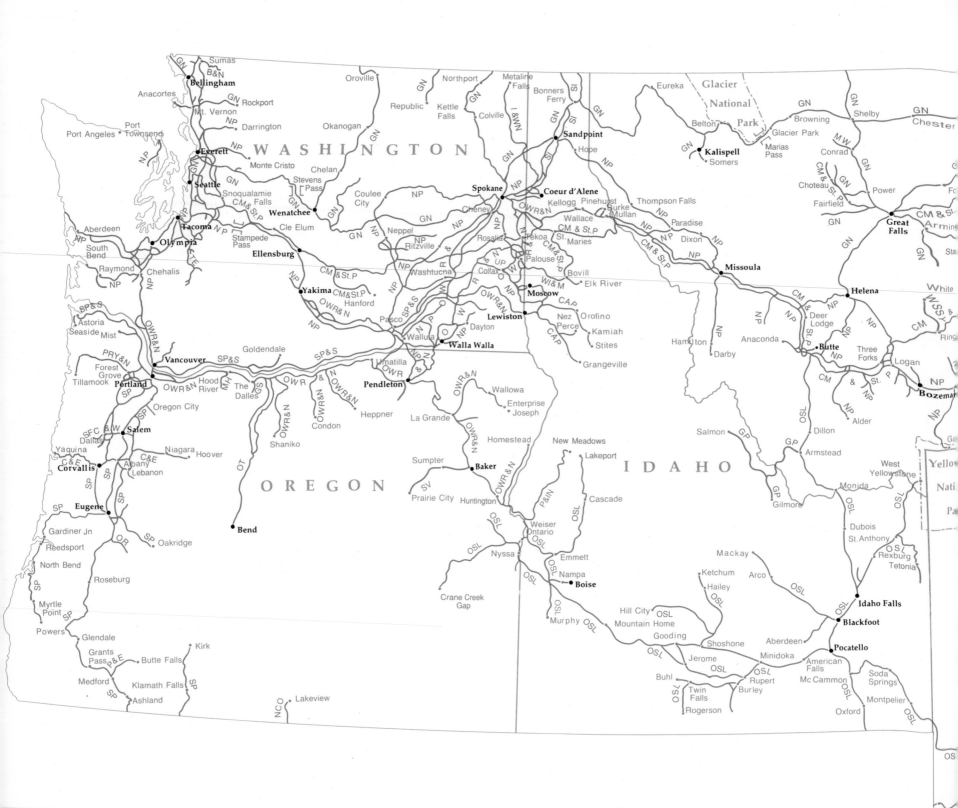

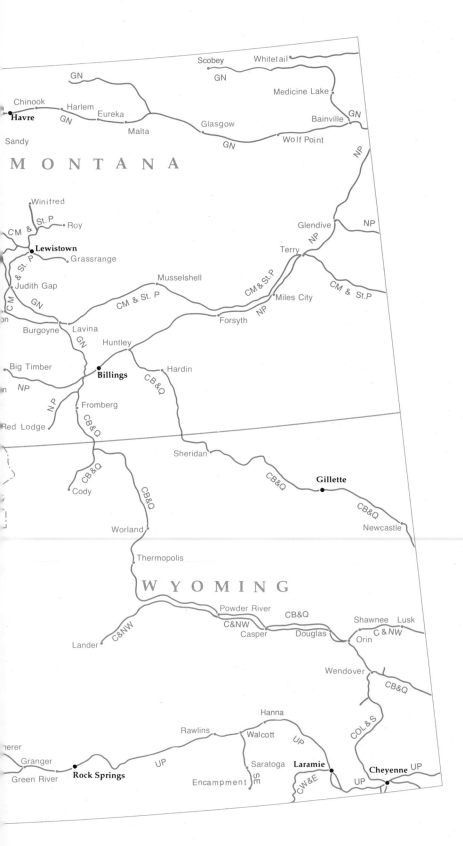

Railroad Signatures

Across the Pacific Northwest: ca. 1916
(Exclusive of Logging and Electric Interurban Railroads)

Bellingham and Northern	B&N
Camas Prairie	CAP
Chicago and North Western	C&NW
Chicago, Burlington and Quincy	CB&Q
Chicago, Milwaukee and St. Paul	CM&St.P
Colorado, Wyoming and Eastern	CW&E
Corvallis and Eastern	C&E
Gilmore and Pittsburgh	GP
Great Northern	GN
Great Southern	GS
Idaho and Washington Northern	I & WN
Mount Hood	MH
Nevada-California-Oregon	NCO
Northern Pacific	NP
Oregon Short Line	OSL
Oregon Trunk	OT
Oregon-Washington Railroad and Navigation Company	OWR & N
Pacific and Eastern	P&E
Pacific and Idaho Northern	P&IN
Pacific Railway and Navigation Company	PRY&N
Salem, Falls City and Western	SFC&W
Saratoga and Encampment	SE
Southern Pacific	SP
Spokane International	SI
Spokane, Portland and Seattle	SP&S
Sumpter Valley	SV
Tacoma Eastern	TE
Union Pacific	UP
Washington, Idaho and Montana	WI&M
White Sulphur Springs and Yellowstone Park	WSSY

▲
N

A vivid illustration typical of railroad art during the 1920s depicts the Great Northern corridor through the Cascade Range. Mount Index is prominent in the background. Courtesy Richard Piper.

Railroad Signatures across the Pacific Northwest

CARLOS A. SCHWANTES

University of Washington Press *Seattle & London*

Railroad Signatures across the Pacific Northwest is published with the assistance of a generous grant from Burlington Northern.

Copyright © 1993 by the University of Washington Press
Second printing (pbk.), 1996
Designed by Audrey Meyer
Endpaper maps by Allan Jokisaari
Printed in Hong Kong by C & C Offset Printing Co., Ltd.

All rights reserved. No part of this publication may be reproduced or transmitted in any form or by any means, electronic or mechanical, including photocopy, recording, or any information storage or retrieval system, without permission in writing from the publisher.

Library of Congress Cataloging-in-Publication Data
Schwantes, Carlos A., 1945–
Railroad signatures across the Pacific Northwest /
Carlos A. Schwantes
     p. cm.
Includes bibliographical references and index.
ISBN 0–295–97535–0 (alk. paper)
1. Railroads—Pacific, Northwest. I. Title
TF23.7.S39   1993   93–6505
385'.09795—dc20   CIP

The paper used in this publication meets the minimum requirements of American National Standard for Information Sciences—Permanence of Paper for Printed Library Materials, ANSI Z39.48–1984. ∞

UNKNOWN PLACES *in* IDAHO

UNION PACIFIC SYSTEM THE OVERLAND ROUTE

UNION PACIFIC SYSTEM

This Union Pacific pamphlet urging tourists to explore unknown corners of Idaho is typical of the attractive travel brochures of the 1920s and 1930s. Union Pacific Museum.

*To four friends
who have influenced
my interest in
transportation history:*

Richard L. Day
William S. Greever
Alfred Runte
W. Thomas White

*M*ost railroad publications
emphasized national parks, but
this brochure promotes national
forest vacations. Note the bear
motif that was popular in tourist
promotions of the 1920s and 1930s.
Minnesota Historical Society.

This popular Milwaukee Road brochure shows a settler plowing gold coins from the fertile Montana soil. University of Montana.

The colorful cover of a Southern Pacific brochure advertised tourism at Crater Lake National Park in 1916. California State Railroad Museum.

CRATER LAKE

OREGON'S Mountain Playground

SOUTHERN PACIFIC

Contents

"One of America's Fine Trains"

NORTHERN PACIFIC
YELLOWSTONE PARK LINE

The North Coast Limited
Silver Anniversary Year

The Northern Pacific issued an elaborate brochure to celebrate the silver anniversary of its North Coast Limited in the mid-1920s. Minnesota Historical Society.

In crowded St. Louis I had never felt so close to America as I did now on this pathless plain. I knew that as I touched the steel linking one rail to another, I was linking myself to the new country and building my own solid road to a new life.
—Stoyan Christowe, My American Pilgrimage *(1947)*

Preface

MANY BOOKS ABOUT RAILROADS concentrate on locomotives. What follows is not a book about railroad engines but about railroads *as engines* of regional development and social change. I approach the subject from the perspective of a student of the Pacific Northwest rather than that of a specialist in railroad or business history. Train buffs will look in vain for extended discussions of equipment and technology, yet I do hope that *Railroad Signatures across the Pacific Northwest* captures for all readers the human drama of a complex subject.

My approach probably reflects the way I was introduced to railroad history some forty summers ago in Wilmington, North Carolina. After dinner at my grandparents' home we often adjourned to the front porch in search of ways to make a muggy evening tolerable. Mostly we spent our time talking and swinging and waiting for a breeze, or perhaps for one of the thunderstorms that brought to the region of the lower Cape Fear River spectacular displays of lightning, torrential rains, and a measure of relief from the heat. My grandfather was a source of knowledge about many things that interested small boys. Together with his father and brother he had once worked for the Atlantic Coast Line Railroad. Years before I was born, my grand-

father had been a member of a "wrecking crew" whose job it was to reopen the tracks following a derailment. When the great shopmen's strike of 1922 prematurely ended his railroading career, he became a policeman, detective, and finally chief of police in Wilmington. I remember Granddaddy Casteen as a gifted checkers player and storyteller; I could never beat him at either one.

Wilmington in the 1950s was still a railroad town, home of the Atlantic Coast Line until the company did an unthinkable thing and moved its headquarters to Jacksonville, Florida, in 1961. Neighbors on both sides of my grandparents had worked for the Coast Line, and much of our evening's conversation naturally turned to railroading or detective work. If there was some sort of connection between my grandfather's elaborate, often humorous accounts of police work and my career as historian, I could never prove it, although I am still partial to history as a well-crafted piece of detection.

My early interest in railroads lingered and grew. It could not have been otherwise. The backyard of my parents' home in Greenfield, Indiana, abutted the main line of the Pennsylvania Railroad between New York City and St. Louis. Every morning a parade of streamlined passenger trains sped west to St. Louis, and every afternoon the parade headed in the opposite direction. Never could I have imagined then that those tracks would be ripped up in the 1980s, leaving only a weed-covered embankment to remind me that the all-Pullman Spirit of St. Louis once sped the Who's Who of America past my backyard. Over breakfast in the dining car such folk may have discussed the war in Korea, debated whether President Truman was right to fire General MacArthur, and speculated on Henry J. Kaiser's latest automobile venture. Or, when conversation flagged, they may have casually wondered what kind of people lived in the cities and towns bisected by Pennsylvania Railroad tracks across central Indiana.

Never once did it occur to me to ponder whether we lived on the right or wrong side of the tracks. I only felt fortunate to have a front-row seat from which to view all the drama of what John Stilgoe would later call the Metropolitan Corridor.[1] From that vantage point I witnessed the railroad industry's historic transition from steam to diesel motive power and the slow decline of its passenger service.

In October 1957 I made a trip to Block's department store in Indianapolis and acquired book number one for my personal library: Lucius Beebe and Charles Clegg's *Age of Steam*.[2] Fifteen dollars for a single book seemed like a staggering sum to a twelve year old. During the intervening years I have continued to add transportation books to my library—often wishing that they still sold for as little as fifteen dollars—as well as an eclectic and seemingly unending stream of notes to my file cabinets. Here I must pause to emphasize the encompassing term *transportation* as distinct from *railroad*. I have always enjoyed traveling by passenger train, but a flight from Miami to Rio de Janeiro in 1952 to visit my paternal grandparents introduced me to the romance of winging over Amazon jungles on Aerovias Brasil's DC-4 at a time when air travel was still a luxury and an adventure. Because no one then was worried about air piracy, pilots still invited children into the cockpit to help "fly" the plane.

This delightful experience, like others I have mentioned, invariably influenced my thinking.

Quite simply, *Railroad Signatures across the Pacific Northwest* seeks to capture the impact of railroads on everyday life in one region of the United States within the context of competing modes of transportation. At one time I thought I wanted to write a social history of the American passenger train during the early automobile age, but with some encouragement from Julidta Tarver of the University of Washington Press, my research finally yielded a more encompassing study that combined my love of Pacific Northwest history with that of railroads and other forms of transportation. In later chapters I do devote more attention to passenger than to freight service, but that is because after 1920 most citizens evaluated the impact of railroads on their lives mainly in terms of passenger trains.

Railroad Signatures is not meant to be a definitive history of Pacific Northwest transportation but rather a work of interpretation and synthesis. It could not have been anything else and remained readable. According to one survey more than five hundred railroad companies were incorporated in Washington alone between 1860 and 1948.[3] I would not propose to provide detailed histories for even a fraction of these carriers; I do, however, take full responsibility for my interpretations and for any errors or omissions that may appear in this book.

The curiosity first aroused in that porch swing in North Carolina has taken me to many places and caused me to pile up a mountain of intellectual debts that now need to be acknowledged. Thanks go first to students in my history classes. For a variety of reasons I am also indebted to Judith Austin, Elizabeth Jacox, and Merle Wells of the Idaho State Historical Society; Lawrence Dodd, Marilyn Sparks, and G. Thomas Edwards of Whitman College; James P. Ronda of the University of Tulsa; Lory Morrow, Rebecca Kohl, and Dave Walter of the Montana Historical Society; Dale L.

Johnson of the University of Montana; Susan Seyl and Elizabeth Winroth of the Oregon Historical Society; Earl Pomeroy, Fraser J. Cocks III, and James D. Fox of the University of Oregon; William G. Robbins and Thomas C. McClintock of Oregon State University; Robert E. Burke and Richard Engeman of the University of Washington; David Nicandri and Edward Nolan of the Washington State Historical Society; W. Thomas White of the James Jerome Hill Reference Library; and Terry Abraham of the University of Idaho.

I further appreciate the help of David Farmer and Dawn Letson of the DeGolyer Library of Southern Methodist University; Kathey Swan of the Denver Public Library; Ruth Ellen Bauer, Dallas R. Lindgren, and Ruby Shields of the Minnesota Historical Society; Mark J. Cedeck of the St. Louis Mercantile Library Association; Paul Woehrmann, Thomas Altmann, Sandy Broder, and Jim Scribbins of the Milwaukee Public Library; Ellen Schwartz and Blaine P. Lamb of the California State Railroad Museum; Christine Droll of the Oakland Museum's Art Department; Don Snoddy of the Union Pacific Museum; Don Hofsommer of St. Cloud State University; Jonathan Dembo of the Cincinnati Historical Society; Terrence M. Cole of the University of Alaska, Fairbanks; Richard Orsi of California State University, Hayward; Leonard Arrington of Salt Lake City; and two aviation professionals, Ray Arnold and Christian Zimmermann, met through the Depot Institute of Cascade, Idaho.

Working with yet another book with my many friends at the University of Washington Press has been a genuine pleasure. In particular, I want to thank Don Ellegood, director; Naomi Pascal, editor-in-chief; Julidta Tarver, managing editor, who patiently oversaw this project from beginning to end; and Audrey Meyer, art director, who did a splendid job of combining prose and illustrations into a truly beautiful book. In addition, Carol Zabilski, associate editor of the University of Wash-

ington's *Pacific Northwest Quarterly*, deserves praise for sculpting my often unruly prose into final form.

Richard Maxwell Brown of the University of Oregon history department made it possible for me to spend the summer of 1981 in Eugene teaching a class and going through the university's large collection of railroad materials. A research grant from the Idaho Humanities Council initiated the writing of *Railroad Signatures* and enabled me to share early findings with audiences in Cascade, Boise, and Pocatello. The Idaho State Board of Education generously provided funds for a reduced teaching load during the spring semester of 1991 and for research travel. Once again the University of Idaho's John Calhoun Smith Memorial Fund provided the money necessary to finish the project.

As the book was ready to go to the printer, I was surprised and gratified when Burlington Northern provided a generous grant to the University of Washington Press to help with the publication of *Railroad Signatures across the Pacific Northwest*. Their interest in the region's variegated railroad heritage, not just in the history of Burlington Northern and its predecessor companies, is both commendable and magnanimous.

Michael Walsh, former chairman of the Union Pacific Railroad, gave generously of his time during a visit to the University of Idaho and later arranged for me to visit the Harriman Dispatching Center in Omaha. Over the years I have also developed an enormous debt of gratitude to numerous unsung railroaders, from ticket agents and telegraphers to car inspectors and locomotive engineers, who shared with me stories from their daily work lives. They helped to strengthen my determination to keep focused on the social history of railroading.

I thank the University of Idaho administration for continuing to provide me a congenial atmosphere in which to teach and write. Without support from Kent Hackmann, chair of the history department; Doyle E. Anderegg, associate dean of the College of Letters and Science; Kurt Olsson, dean of the College of Letters and Science; Thomas O. Bell, provost; and Elisabeth Zinser, president, this book would not have been possible. *Railroad Signatures across the Pacific Northwest* is one of four book projects sponsored by the University of Idaho's Institute for Pacific Northwest Studies.

Allan Jokisaari of the University of Idaho's Cart-O-Graphics Lab prepared the two large maps that appear as endpapers, and Nancy Dafoe of the History Department helped me in an incredible variety of ways. Finally, I want to thank my colleagues Lawrence Merk and James Toomey for inviting me to test my ideas in their "World of Corporate Business" class.

I am especially indebted to four scholars who have in a variety of ways encouraged my study of transportation history. Richard L. Day is a retired professor of geography at the University of Idaho; W. Thomas White, curator at the James Jerome Hill Reference Library, helped make it possible for me to travel to St. Paul for research in the papers of James J. Hill and his son Louis Hill; Alfred Runte broadened my horizons by helping me see the relationship between railroads and the national parks. My predecessor in the University of Idaho history department, William S. Greever, has been an unfailing source of professional support. He kindly shared his large private library of railroadiana with me. It is to these four friends that *Railroad Signatures across the Pacific Northwest* is dedicated.

The Milwaukee Road often paused to salute its technological prowess. This brochure featuring a bipolar electric locomotive appeared in 1936. Only one of the massive engines survived: it is preserved in the National Museum of Transport near St. Louis. Denver Public Library, Western History Department.

Railroad Signatures across the Pacific Northwest

The pioneer railroads had to bring the people who furnished the traffic; had to open up the state's first coal mines; set the pace in lumber operations, point out the way to apply irrigation principles, donate manufacturing sites to encourage the building of coast seaports, build and maintain the first line of grain warehouses, exploit the possibilities of foreign trade and give financial encouragement to the first struggling shippers. Then, in order that nothing in the way of paternalism might be overlooked, the earlier railroads took complete charge of the state's legislative efforts and even indicated where the streets in the larger cities should run so as not to interfere with railroad terminals.

—M. M. Mattison, *"Rail Transportation in Washington,"*
Pacific Monthly *(April 1908)*

See all the Northern Pacific mountains you can on your journey, for they are unsurpassed anywhere in the world! Twenty-eight ranges are visible from your train window—the same vast mountains that Lewis and Clark overcame, rich now in the lore of pioneer days in the Northwest, wearing the mantle of glamor that gold prospector, railroad builder, and "dude" rancher have put upon their mighty shoulders!

—Northern Pacific: 2000 *Miles of Scenic Beauty ([1931])*

This is what the railroad has done. It has lengthened life and shortened space.
Space has been cut down by steam and our lives have been relatively lengthened.
—James J. Hill in Pacific Monthly *(January 1909)*

Introduction: Railroad Time and Space in the New Northwest

This classic photograph of the Northern Pacific's luxurious North Coast Limited dates from the early twentieth century: the train was hurrying west from Portland to the ferry connection at Goble, where it would cross the Columbia River and continue north to Tacoma and Seattle. University of Oregon, Angelus 1761.

ANYONE WHO HAS TRAVELED east along the Columbia River from Portland will recall a mountain-and-water landscape so awe-inspiring that Congress in 1986 designated it the Columbia River Gorge Scenic Area. Rand McNally's *Road Atlas* for 1991 named the portion of Interstate 84 through the gorge one of America's eight Top Scenic Routes. No other stretch of superhighway was included in this most select list. Occasional low clouds and mist that shroud distant promontories only heighten the gorge's appeal for romantics inclined to use words like *brooding* and *mysterious* to describe the landscape.

The ninety-mile-long stretch of river is equally rich in history: rocky palisades that drop abruptly four hundred feet or more to the water's edge presented one final obstacle to pioneers who first headed their covered wagons west along the Oregon Trail in the 1840s. With the long-sought promised land of the Willamette Valley lying just beyond the Cascade Range, would-be settlers who had already endured nearly two thousand miles of challenges were forced to confront the treacherous Columbia. Waters that drained from an area larger than France squeezed between the confining walls of the gorge, and the resulting maelstrom forced immigrants either to risk their lives in makeshift rafts or to

detour south of Mount Hood along a primitive toll road. Even experienced rivermen hired by early-day fur companies sometimes miscalculated and drowned in the Columbia's massive falls, chutes, and whirlpools. The challenge was no less great for railroad builders in the early 1880s, who used ropes to lower Chinese laborers down towering rock walls to drill and blast a narrow ledge for tracks of the Oregon Railway & Navigation Company.

The Columbia Gorge probably witnessed more key events in the region's transportation history than any comparable site. Not many of the "first" or "most significant" developments are today obvious from Interstate 84; some are not even commemorated with roadside markers. Yet it was in the Columbia Gorge that workmen hammered into place the wooden tracks of a crude portage line in 1851. That first railway ran a short distance along the Washington bank of the river and was designed to carry passengers and freight around a dangerous stretch of white water known as the Cascades. Only gradually did a network of tracks emerge that was independent of portage lines and the large fleet of steamboats that once plied the Columbia and other major waterways.

Railroad tracks, whether fashioned from wood, iron, or steel, remained an inconspicuous addition

*T*rains of the Spokane, Portland & Seattle Railway followed the north bank through the Columbia Gorge. The photographer took this picture near Cascades, Washington, where a portage railroad once linked steamboats on two separate segments of the river. Tracks of the rival Oregon Railroad & Navigation Company, a Union Pacific subsidiary, extend along the opposite bank. Oregon Historical Society, 67347, File 891-C-1.

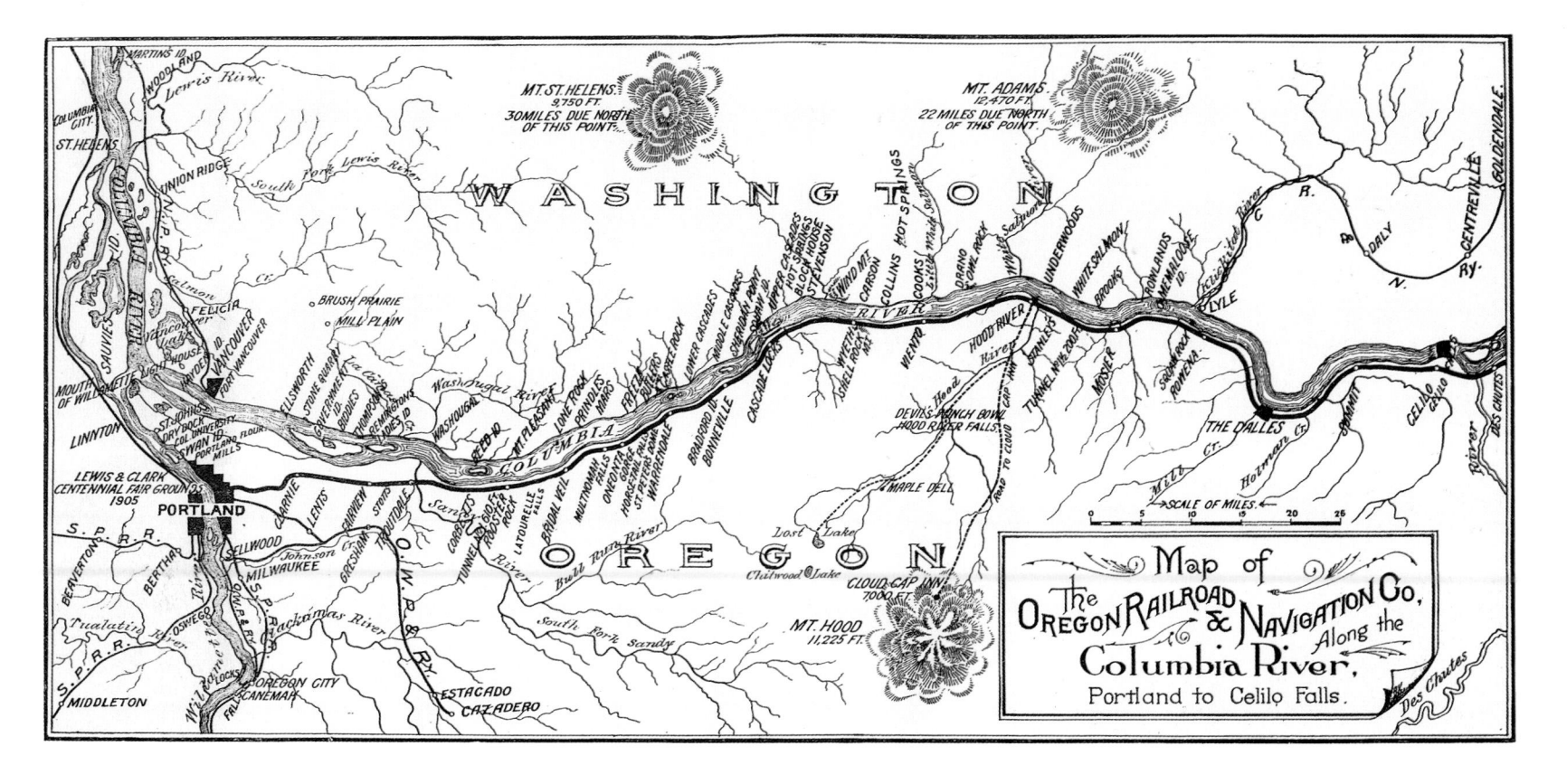

A *turn-of-the-century map shows the route of the Oregon Railroad & Navigation Company through the Columbia River Gorge. The company succeeded the venerable Oregon Railway & Navigation Company in the late 1890s. Oregon Historical Society, 086217.*

to the regional landscape until the late 1870s. Not until a frenzy of tracklaying gripped the region between 1880 and 1893 did railroads write clearly legible signatures across the Pacific Northwest. When a nationwide depression temporarily halted construction in mid-1893 and ended the first railway age, an 8,000-mile network of tracks stretched across Oregon, Washington, Idaho, and Montana. The Pacific Northwest's second railway age lasted from the return of prosperity in 1897 until America entered World War I in early 1917. During those two decades workmen spiked another 8,000 miles of new line into place and upgraded numerous older sections. The region's first railway age emphasized construction of new lines and spurred the rise of whole new cities and industries. The second emphasized improved plants and equipment and was a time of growing, and ultimately suffocating, public

regulation of railroads. During both ages, railroads publicized the Pacific Northwest as a promising field for investment, settlement, and tourism, and in that way they functioned as engines of empire.

The pattern of railroad signatures was never random. Where practicable, builders followed the banks of rivers and lakes. The region's five historic trunk lines were all synonymous with waterways: the Southern Pacific with the Willamette River; the Northern Pacific with the Yellowstone, Clark Fork, and Yakima rivers; the Union Pacific with the Umatilla and Columbia rivers and the vast Snake River plain of southern Idaho; the Great Northern with the Flathead, Kootenai, Wenatchee, and Snohomish rivers and with Puget Sound; and the Chicago, Milwaukee, St. Paul & Pacific with the Musselshell, St. Joe, and Yakima rivers. The main body of water to figure in the strategies of all transcontinental railroad builders was the Pacific Ocean. Its name appeared in the corporate titles of all but one northern trunk line as well as in that of the Canadian Pacific Railway, which extended from Montreal to Vancouver.

To railroad builders, some rivers of the Pacific Northwest appeared totally uncooperative: waters of the Salmon or River of No Return rushed through the mountains of central Idaho with such force that they turned back the explorers Lewis and Clark in the early 1800s as well as every railroad builder who later contemplated a line through the river's narrow confines. The Snake did likewise as it churned through Hells Canyon, and that formidable barrier was a primary reason why no railroad line ever ran the length of the Gem State. Waterways played a key role in track location, but more than topography alone determined the shape of railroad signatures. They reflected the aspirations of metropolitan centers like Portland, Seattle, and Spokane; they were sensitive to the location of valuable mineral deposits, such as copper in Butte, Montana, silver in the Coeur d'Alene Valley of northern Idaho, and coal in the Cascade foothills east of Seattle and Tacoma; and they defined areas of large-scale agricultural production.

Finally, the signatures reflected the egos of a handful of powerful railroad builders. Historians in recent years have become reluctant to attribute too much influence to a few "great men," yet it was undeniable that three men above all others—Henry Villard, James J. Hill, and Edward H. Harriman—shaped the modern Pacific Northwest by the way they wrote their corporate signatures in steel. The fact that Burlington Northern freight trains thunder through the Columbia Gorge along the north bank of the river while Union Pacific freights follow the south bank reveals as much about individual egos as about geography and geology. In the early twentieth century, Hill supported construction of an expensive new railroad between Portland and Spokane in an effort to wrest a portion of Oregon's growing commerce from his arch-rival, Harriman, who dominated the state's transportation at that time by controlling both the Union Pacific and Southern Pacific systems. When Harriman used his ownership of the little-used and largely forgotten portage line at the Cascades to block Hill, lawyers for the rail titans waged a vigorous battle that ended in Hill's favor.

Railroad construction slowed noticeably by the eve of World War I. With the onset of a new age of competition, highway engineers used tax money from an increasingly automobile-minded public to write bold new signatures in concrete and asphalt. Once again the Columbia River Gorge was the setting for momentous developments: the first section of the Columbia River Highway opened in 1915, and seven years later the engineering marvel connected Portland and The Dalles. Construction of the present superhighway through the gorge in the 1960s destroyed portions of the early road. Significant sections nonetheless remain intact and usable by any motorist willing to slow down and seek out the Historic Columbia River Highway that parallels parts of Interstate 84 and provides entrance to a series of moss-and-fern grottos and waterfalls that delight hikers and landscape photographers. Along one twelve-mile stretch of the old route, eleven waterfalls are either visible or readily accessible to motorists. In some places the sound of rushing water competes with that of Union Pacific freights rumbling along nearby tracks.

Time: Starvation Creek and Days of Two Noons

CONSIDER THE LITTLE STREAM that flows unnoticed beneath Interstate 84 and the Union Pacific tracks about ten miles east of the town of Cascade Locks.

A Union Pacific train passes the Pillars of Hercules in the scenic Columbia River gorge in this undated photograph. Union Pacific Museum, 7000043.

Multnomah Falls is a veil of water and mist that drops 620 feet, more than three times the height of Niagara Falls. For years Union Pacific passenger trains paused or slowed at the base of the scenic wonder to afford travelers a better look. Union Pacific Museum, 700036.

*Carleton Watkins photographed
workers cutting through a
mountain of snow to clear Oregon
Railway & Navigation tracks
between Rooster Rock and Oneonta
Gorge in the harsh winter of
1884–85. DeGolyer Library, AG
82 232.26723.*

The name Starvation Creek gives only a hint of the drama that took place there in the winter of 1884, an event that demonstrated how railroads redefined something so basic as the meaning of time in a pioneer society. In their passenger service, railroads brought to everyday life in the Pacific Northwest a degree of discipline previously unknown. Where stagecoach lines had shut down with winter snows and waited for spring thaws to reopen roads and trails, railways sought to master nature by using armies of men and a variety of special equipment to battle ice and snow. Sometimes, however, they lost the struggle, as they did in the Columbia River gorge in 1884.

On December 19 a blizzard piled up massive snowdrifts across the newly completed tracks of the Oregon Railway & Navigation Company and trapped the Pacific Express, the overland limited that ran daily between St. Paul and Portland. The train was due to arrive in the Oregon metropolis by midmorning, but instead it braked to an unscheduled stop in the Columbia Gorge. Seemingly within seconds, blowing snow buried both engines and partially covered the rest of the train. It was impossible to return to Hood River, only ten miles back, much less continue fifty miles ahead to Portland, where many of the 148 passengers expected to spend their Christmas holidays. They might just as well have been stranded on the remote plains of eastern Montana. At least the abrupt stop injured no one, and there was food enough aboard for the day's meals. The conductor Edward Lyons rummaged through the baggage car, where he located three cases of oysters, two quarters of beef, some mutton, and about seventy-five jackrabbits.

Initial efforts to dig out the train failed, but

during a lull in the storm, crewmen succeeded in backing the cars a few hundred feet onto a small wooden trestle where they hoped passengers were out of danger from avalanches. As the fury of the storm increased again, blowing and drifting snow prevented plows from reaching the stranded train from either Portland or The Dalles. On December 22, a dwindling food supply forced Lyons to send nearly every able-bodied man out into the blizzard, each to seek his own safety. All survived the arduous trek to Troutdale, where rescuers from nearby Portland met them. Men on skis managed to pull heavy sleds of food to feed the remaining passengers.

Christmas came and went. Holiday dinner consisted of bacon, beans, canned fruit, pickles, and coffee. Rescue efforts continued around the clock, but progress was agonizingly slow. Drifts topped fifty feet in places, and snow mixed with ice formed a solid wall across the tracks between Multnomah Falls and Oneonta Gorge. Plows derailed and a locomotive tipped over, fatally crushing an engineer. An army of a thousand men recruited in Portland used picks and shovels to hack and dig away at snow and ice walls. New Year's Day passed, but the train remained snowbound until the weather abruptly warmed a few days later. Shortly after midnight on the morning of January 8, the remaining passengers finally steamed into Portland. They arrived almost three weeks late.

At the time of the 1884 blizzard, through train service between the Pacific Northwest and the East had been in operation slightly longer than a year. Before that, winter had simply brought normal life to a halt in much of the nation's Far Corner. Miners endured a bleak life in isolated camps and occasionally suffered from scurvy as a result of diets lacking in fresh fruits and vegetables. There was joyful weeping in the streets of Virginia City, Montana, in May 1864 when the first wagonload of flour arrived after a five-month hiatus caused by snow blocking

Rocky Mountain passes.[1] Even in Portland, the region's commercial metropolis, the pace of life slowed noticeably during winter months.

Northwesterners had once reckoned travel mainly in terms of seasons: in the 1840s and 1850s emigrants headed their covered wagons west from the valley of the Missouri River in spring when grasses of the Great Plains were lush and green. They fattened their draft animals in anticipation of the mountains and deserts ahead. They hoped to reach the Continental Divide at South Pass by midsummer and the Willamette Valley by early fall. The region's rural residents continued to measure time by the larger rhythms of life, by seasonal changes, sunrise and sunset, and Sunday as the start of a new week. Preindustrial societies did not ordinarily require more precise measurements. Although Pacific Northwest residents eventually refined their concept of time to include hours, railroads demanded even

Two locomotives of the Oregon Short Line struggle through winter snows of eastern Idaho near Monida Pass to haul a Union Pacific passenger train north to Butte from Pocatello. Idaho State Historical Society, 74-78.41K.

Because of a breach of the industrial discipline that safe operation of railroads required, two Northern Pacific trains met head-on in a minor accident near Pullman, Washington, in 1892. Washington State University, 78-361.

shorter intervals. They required people to think in terms of minutes, a measure that clearly defined the pace of life in industrial America.

In the Pacific Northwest, and elsewhere in the United States during the 1880s, the typical railroad consisted of a single track with sidings (or turnouts) spaced every few miles to permit trains to pass one another. Safe operations demanded that conductors and engineers follow thick books of rules, employee timetables, and special orders; the meeting places of trains had to be designated precisely in hours and minutes to prevent collisions. By the early 1920s an army of approximately four thousand inspectors and assistants regularly checked the watches of a million railroaders a year in the United States and Canada to maintain the margin of safety.[2]

Accident-free operation further demanded that crews synchronize their watches at the beginning of each run. For that reason the boundaries between standard time zones invariably coincided with places where train crews changed. In the Pacific Northwest, railroad towns like Troy, Montana; Hope, Idaho; and Huntington, Oregon, marked the boundaries between Mountain and Pacific time. Huntington still does today. Railroads also standardized to the minute the distance between such metropolitan centers as Portland and San Francisco. In 1905, for instance, the Southern Pacific's Shasta Express required exactly seventeen hours and five minutes to cover the 772 miles that separated the two cities. After standardizing distance in terms of hours and minutes, carriers took all steps necessary to maintain their schedules even in the face of unpredictable winter storms.

Time zones themselves were a railroad invention. They did not exist prior to November 18, 1883, the "day of two noons," when many influential railroads of the United States arbitrarily resolved fifty-six

standards of time into just four standard zones without any authorization from either state or federal governments. Railroads centering on Portland waited until Sunday, December 16, to adopt the new Pacific time. In either case, until late 1883 no meaningful time standard prevailed in America. A traveler going from Eastport, Maine, to San Francisco had to change his watch twenty times during the trip. At least twenty-seven local times existed in Michigan and twenty-three in Indiana.

As long as individual railroad companies operated their trains only short distances, time differences were of little consequence. But as railroads grew longer and more complex and their trains passed through major cities observing different standards of time, confusion resulted. Especially was that true for passengers trying to make connections between railroads that used time standards based on different cities. Trains running between Omaha and Chicago in 1870 used Chicago time, which was twenty-three minutes later than Omaha. Those between Omaha and Cheyenne operated by Union Pacific time, which was eleven minutes later than Omaha time. Trains south to Kansas City followed yet a third standard. When an employee asked about the difference between Union Pacific time and that of its headquarters city, he was told that the railroad followed the clock in its telegraph office in Omaha, which was originally on local time. However, "the clock has not been set for three years and during that time it has gained 11 minutes."[3]

After railroads adopted standard time, there were inevitable holdouts. Some ministers objected to railroads taking unto themselves a power reserved only to God. An Indianapolis newspaper complained, "The sun is no longer boss of the job. People, 55,000,000 of them, must eat, sleep and work as well as travel by railroad time."[4] The railroads' reordering of time perhaps symbolized better than anything else the far-reaching changes they were capable of promoting.

What Time Do You Have?

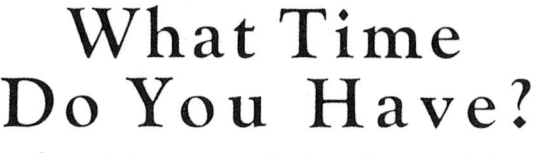

If you ask that question of Conductor Thomas or Engineer Sullivan, of the Rock Island "Midcontinent Special," they will both answer: "Hamilton time." These veterans in railroad service know that Hamilton time means accurate time; Hamilton, to them, is just another word for accuracy.

And that's the way most railroad men feel about it. They know that Hamilton is all that a railroad watch should be—a timepiece of accuracy, sturdiness and dependability. They know that Hamilton embodies every worthwhile feature known to watchmaking science, even though its makers never boastfully "blow smoke" about it.

When you need a watch—and perhaps during 1928 you will want to make a change—insist on owning a Hamilton. That is the best way of insuring yourself watch satisfaction. Write for a copy of the new Hamilton Time Book and folder dealing with the various railroad models. You will find them both mighty useful.

HAMILTON WATCH COMPANY
999 Wheatland Avenue, Lancaster, Penna., U. S. A.

Hamilton railroad models are now available fitted with either the famous Hamilton 992 movement, 21 jewels, adjusted to five positions, or the Hamilton 950 movement, 23 jewels, adjusted to five positions. Your jeweler will be glad to show you any of these models—in filled white, green or yellow gold.

"The Railroad Timekeeper of America"

Our Advertisers are Patronizing Your Magazine

An advertisement for Hamilton watches in the mid-1920s emphasized the importance of accurate timekeeping. Minnesota Historical Society, Great Northern Railway Company Records, 19.A.10.3B.